FREE Study Skills DVD

Dear Customer,

Thank you for your purchase from Mometrix! We consider it an honor and a privilege that you have purchased our product and we want to ensure your satisfaction.

As a way of showing our appreciation and to help us better serve you, we have developed a Study Skills DVD that we would like to give you for <u>FREE</u>. This DVD covers our *best practices* for getting ready for your exam, from how to use our study materials to how to best prepare for the day of the test.

All that we ask is that you email us with feedback that would describe your experience so far with our product. Good, bad, or indifferent, we want to know what you think!

To get your FREE Study Skills DVD, email <u>freedvd@mometrix.com</u> with *FREE STUDY SKILLS DVD* in the subject line and the following information in the body of the email:

- The name of the product you purchased.
- Your product rating on a scale of 1-5, with 5 being the highest rating.
- Your feedback. It can be long, short, or anything in between. We just want to know your impressions and experience so far with our product. (Good feedback might include how our study material met your needs and ways we might be able to make it even better. You could highlight features that you found helpful or features that you think we should add.)
- Your full name and shipping address where you would like us to send your free DVD.

If you have any questions or concerns, please don't hesitate to contact me directly.

Thanks again!

Sincerely,

Jay Willis
Vice President
<u>jay.willis@mometrix.com</u>
1-800-673-8175

Series 65
Exam
Practice Questions

Series 65 Practice Tests & Review for the
Uniform Investment Adviser Law Examination

Written and edited by the Mometrix Financial Industry Certification Test Team

Printed in the United States of America

This paper meets the requirements of ANSI/NISO Z39.48-1992 (Permanence of Paper).

Mometrix offers volume discount pricing to institutions. For more information or a price quote, please contact our sales department at sales@mometrix.com or 888-248-1219.

Mometrix Media LLC is not affiliated with or endorsed by any official testing organization. All organizational and test names are trademarks of their respective owners.

ISBN 13: 978-1-63094-609-8
ISBN 10: 1-63094-609-5

DEAR FUTURE EXAM SUCCESS STORY

First of all, **THANK YOU** for purchasing Mometrix study materials!

Second, congratulations! You are one of the few determined test-takers who are committed to doing whatever it takes to excel on your exam. **You have come to the right place.** We developed these practice tests with one goal in mind: to deliver you the best possible approximation of the questions you will see on test day.

Standardized testing is one of the biggest obstacles on your road to success, which only increases the importance of doing well in the high-pressure, high-stakes environment of test day. Your results on this test could have a significant impact on your future, and these practice tests will give you the repetitions you need to build your familiarity and confidence with the test content and format to help you achieve your full potential on test day.

Your success is our success

We would love to hear from you! If you would like to share the story of your exam success or if you have any questions or comments in regard to our products, please contact us at **800-673-8175** or **support@mometrix.com**.

Thanks again for your business and we wish you continued success!

Sincerely,
The Mometrix Test Preparation Team

TABLE OF CONTENTS

Practice Test #1

1. Which is a primary risk to an investor's "purchasing power"?

    a. Low interest rates
    b. Equity volatility
    c. Inflation
    d. Deflation

2. Which of the following is a tool to measure inflation?

    a. The yield curve
    b. The CPI
    c. Food and energy prices
    d. The Discount rate

3. The most used and most well-known leading economic indicator is:

    a. New unemployment claims
    b. Consumer confidence
    c. The S&P 500
    d. The new jobs payroll reports

4. Four consecutive quarters of declining GDP are labeled as:

    a. A depression
    b. A recession
    c. A soft patch
    d. Slowing growth

5. Which of the following are lagging economic indicators?

    a. Personal income levels
    b. Monetary supply (M2)
    c. CPI change
    d. New building permits

6. In a situation where short term interest rates are higher than longer term interest rates, which of the following is true?

    a. The yield curve is inverted and is an indicator of positive economic growth
    b. The yield curve is normal and is an indicator of positive economic growth
    c. The yield curve is inverted and is an indicator of negative economic growth
    d. The yield curve is normal and is an indicator of negative economic growth

7. Two financial ratios, the Current ratio and the Quick ratio, are almost identical except for one key metric. Which of the following is included in the Current ratio, but not the Quick ratio?

    a. Current liabilities
    b. Cash on hand
    c. Inventories
    d. Goodwill

1

8. On an income statement, which of the following is NOT used to calculate operating margin?

    a. Advertising expenses
    b. Depreciation expenses
    c. Cost of goods sold
    d. Interest expenses

9. On a balance sheet, assets are generally one of three types. Which of the following is not a type of asset found on a balance sheet?

    a. Current assets
    b. Fixed assets
    c. Saleable assets
    d. Intangible assets

10. An 8-K filing is which of the following?

    a. An annual report filed by all public companies
    b. A quarterly report filed by public companies
    c. A monthly report filed by public companies
    d. A report of important news before the next scheduled report

11. Which of the following is true about the Price-to-Earnings ratio?

    a. Diluted earnings per share is most important
    b. The dividend payout ratio is most important
    c. It is more important to preferred stock investors than common stock investors
    d. It can fluctuate greatly even when the earnings don't change

12. Calculating the Net Present Value (NPV) is useful in which of the following situations?

    a. Comparing a bond investment to a stock investment
    b. Deciding whether a business investment is a good use of cash
    c. Deciding which of two mutual funds is a better investment
    d. Comparing an investment in a preferred stock to a common stock

13. If your city's average annual income is $52,000, this is which of the "measures of central tendency"?

    a. Median
    b. Mode
    c. Mean
    d. Average

14. Using the analogy of a roller-coaster to discuss the "scariness" of a ride made for kids versus one made for adults (bigger kids), the appropriate measure would be:

    a. Standard deviation
    b. Beta
    c. Systematic risk
    d. Adrenaline response

15. Which of the following investment risks cannot be diversified away?

a. Market risk
b. Event risk
c. Interest rate risk
d. Business risk

16. Investing in zero-coupon treasury bonds eliminates all of the following risks except?

a. Purchasing power risk
b. Reinvestment risk
c. Liquidity risk
d. Political risk

17. Moving money from a savings account paying 1% to invest in an equity mutual fund expected to return 6-8% is an example of what?

a. Greener grass investing
b. Opportunity cost
c. Diversifying systematic risk
d. Avoiding default risk

18. Which of the following is NOT a good strategy to reduce non-systematic risk in a portfolio?

a. Investing in index funds
b. Investing in a Balanced mutual fund
c. Only invest in your own industry that you really understand
d. Investing a portion of your money internationally

19. Which of the following has the most exposure to liquidation priority?

a. Common stockholders
b. Preferred stockholders
c. Bondholders
d. Lien holders

20. Which of the following is not considered a money market security?

a. Treasury Bill
b. Jumbo negotiable certificates of deposit
c. 14-month commercial paper
d. 1-month variable rate demand obligations

21. Advantages of brokered CDs over bank CDs include all of the following except:

a. Greater safety of principal
b. Higher yields
c. Greater liquidity
d. More convenient FDIC insurance

22. Which of the following is not an example of a Tax-Exempt Municipal note?

a. TAN
b. RAN
c. BAN
d. BRAN

23. If you were primarily interested in safety, which municipal bond would you prefer to invest in?

    a. A General Obligation bond
    b. A Revenue bond
    c. A Limited tax GO bond
    d. A Double-barreled bond

24. Which of the following Agency bonds is directly backed by the full faith and credit of the US Government?

    a. Federal National Mortgage Association
    b. Government National Mortgage Association
    c. Federal Home Loan Mortgage Corporation
    d. Student Loan Marketing Association

25. A distinguishing feature of Brady Bonds is that:

    a. They are international bonds of developed countries
    b. There is no currency risk, as they pay in US dollars
    c. They are collateralized by US treasuries
    d. They are immune to political risk

26. A convertible bond's price is most directly influenced by which of the following?

    a. Interest rates
    b. The stock's dividend
    c. The S&P 500
    d. The stock's price

27. If someone recommended buying these bonds through them, you might suspect them of fraud:

    a. Series EE bonds
    b. HH bonds
    c. I bonds
    d. GNMA bonds

28. For a Premium bond, place the yields in the proper order, highest to lowest:

    1. Current yield
    2. Yield to maturity
    3. Coupon yield or stated yield

    a. 1, 2, 3
    b. 2, 1, 3
    c. 3, 1, 2
    d. 3, 2, 1

29. What is another name for the "nominal yield"?

    a. Current yield
    b. Yield to Call
    c. Yield to Maturity
    d. Coupon rate

30. In an environment of steadily rising interest rates, the average investor looking to preserve capital should avoid which of the following investments?

    a. Real estate investment trusts
    b. Long term bonds
    c. Short term bonds
    d. Large cap stocks

31. List the following shares in order from the smallest number to the largest:

        1. Authorized shares
        2. Outstanding shares
        3. Restricted shares

    a. 1, 2, 3
    b. 3, 2, 1
    c. 2, 1, 3
    d. 2, 3, 1

32. What is the proper order of occurrence when a company pays a stock dividend?

        1. The payable date
        2. The declaration date
        3. The record date
        4. The dividend date

    a. 1, 2, 3, 4
    b. 4, 3, 2,
    c. 2, 1, 3, 4
    d. 2, 3, 1

33. Which of the following is NOT a type of preferred stock?

    a. Convertible preferred
    b. Callable preferred
    c. Perpetual preferred
    d. Cumulative preferred

34. If you wanted to secure the option to purchase a stock at a certain price for the longest period of time, you would purchase which of the following?

    a. Warrants
    b. Rights
    c. Options
    d. LEAP options

35. The best definition of an ADR is:

    a. A foreign stock denominated in US Dollars
    b. A foreign stock issued in the US
    c. A foreign stock tradable in the US
    d. A foreign stock that avoids currency risk

36. Which of the following is most likely to be used by a Growth investor?

    a. The Relative Strength indicator
    b. Price-to-Sales ratio
    c. PEG ratio
    d. Tangible book value

37. Which of the following would be of most importance to a value investor?

    a. The PE ratio
    b. The earnings growth of a company
    c. The intrinsic value of a company
    d. The price-to-book ratio

38. The best way to get a discount on mutual funds for a new investor looking to put significant money away over the next 12-18 months is:

    a. Breakpoints
    b. Use B shares
    c. Rights of Accumulation
    d. Letter of Intent

39. Which is not an appropriate method of diversification for a mutual fund?

    a. Industry diversification
    b. Geographic diversification
    c. Demographic diversification
    d. Market cap diversification

40. Which of the following is not regulated under the Investment Company Act of 1940?

    a. Open-end mutual fund companies
    b. Unit Investment Trusts
    c. Private Equity fund
    d. Exchange Traded fund

41. Which of the following is not true of both Exchange Traded Funds and Unit Investment Trusts?

    a. Diversification
    b. Passive management
    c. Instant liquidity
    d. Niche investing opportunities

42. Under what circumstances can you purchase a mutual fund for less than NAV?

    a. At the largest breakpoint
    b. When dividends and capital gains are reinvested
    c. When a closed-end mutual fund trades at a discount
    d. When the POP is less than the NAV

43. Which is the least expensive price at which to buy an open-end mutual fund?

    a. the POP (Public offering price)
    b. the NAV (Net asset value) price
    c. With a Rights of Accumulation breakpoint
    d. With a Letter of Intent breakpoint

44. Which of the following options strategies allows you to make money from a stock going down in price?

1. Buying a call option
2. Selling a call option
3. Buying a put option
4. Selling a put option

a. 1 and 3
b. 2 and 4
c. 1 and 4
d. 2 and 3

45. The standard operating terms of a hedge fund are:

a. 2% and 20%
b Illiquid lockups
c. Only accredited investors
d. All of the above

46. A private equity fund is generally structured as:

a. A hedge fund
b. A limited partnership
c. An especially risky and illiquid hedge fund
d. A private mutual fund limited to accredited investors

47. Which of the following does not have a cash savings feature?

a. Term insurance
b. Whole life insurance
c. Universal life insurance
d. Variable life insurance

48. Which is the best option for someone in need of an income now?

a. Variable annuity
b. Fixed annuity
c. Immediate annuity
d. Equity indexed annuity

49. For someone who is young, needs life insurance, but also wants to invest money, which of the following best meets his or her needs?

a. Term life insurance
b. Variable universal life insurance
c. Equity indexed annuity
d. Universal life insurance

50. For an elderly client who is very risk averse but does not need current income, which is the best solution?

a. Immediate annuity
b. Equity indexed annuity
c. Variable annuity
d. Fixed annuity

51. Which form of business ownership provides the least amount of liability protection?

a. Limited Liability Partnership
b. The S Corporation
c. Sole proprietorship
d. Limited Liability Corporation

52. If the primary concerns are reducing taxation and liability, which ownership structure would be best?

a. Sole proprietorship
b. LLP
c. LLC
d. C Corp

53. For a company looking to raise investment capital, the best structure is:

a. LLP
b. LLC
c. S Corp
d. C Corp

54. In which business structure does one member have a "fiduciary duty" to the other members?

a. LLP
b. LLC
c. S corp
d. C corp

55. In developing a client profile, which is not an important piece of information to gather?

a. Discretionary income
b. Health issues
c. Retirement age
d. Existing assets

56. In developing a client's risk suitability, what is the most important factor?

a. Discretionary income
b. Tax bracket
c. Time horizon
d. Existing assets

57. If a client is in a high tax bracket and nearing retirement, which asset class may make sense?

a. Dividend paying stocks
b. Bond mutual funds
c. REITs
d. Municipal bonds

8

58. For a 60-year-old woman with a low risk tolerance, no investing experience, five years until retirement, and only $50,000 in savings; which investment can we eliminate from recommending?

a. Bond mutual fund
b. Growth and income mutual fund
c. Individual small cap stocks
d. Money market funds

59. Which of the following is a distinguishing feature of Modern Portfolio Theory?

a. It's based on the strong version of Efficient Market Hypothesis
b. It's based on the Capital Asset Pricing Model
c. It's based on portfolio optimization
d. It's based on sector rotation

60. Which form of the Efficient Market Hypothesis says that fundamental analysis CAN, but technical analysis CANNOT, be used to outperform the market?

a. Weak form
b. Semi-Weak form
c. Semi-Strong form
d. Strong form

61. The Capital Asset Pricing Model relies on what key metric to calculate expected return?

a. The Sharpe ratio
b. The risk premium
c. The investment Alpha
d. The risk-free rate

62. A believer in the strong form of the Efficient Market Hypothesis would be likely to employ the following:

a. Sector rotation
b. Strategic asset allocation
c. Tactical asset allocation
d. Strategic technical analysis

63. The buy and hold strategy of investing can best be described as:

a. A value oriented passive strategy
b. An active growth stock strategy
c. Reducing expenses and taxes through exchange traded funds
d. Buying good investments of any style and holding them for the very long term

64. In which of the following is an income investor most likely to be interested when analyzing a stock?

a. The company's balance sheet
b. The short interest
c. The dividend payout ratio
d. The price/earnings multiple

65. A portfolio consisting of 15% Large cap value, 15% Large cap growth, 10% Mid cap, 15% Small cap, 10% High yield bonds, 20% Corporate bonds, 15% International can be said to be:
- a. Diversified
- b. Rebalanced
- c. A Passive investor
- d. Sector rotating

66. If the portfolio from the previous question is now 17% Large cap value, 13% Large cap growth, 11% Mid cap, 17% Small cap, 9% High yield bonds, 16% Corporate bonds, and 17% International, then it should be time for:
- a. Dollar cost averaging
- b. Sector rotation
- c. Rebalancing
- d. Profit taking

67. The time-honored technique of investing a set amount on a regular basis in order to take advantage of the volatility of prices is known as:
- a. Buying low
- b. Dollar cost averaging
- c. Rebalancing
- d. Sector rotation

68. Proper portfolio diversification can reduce all of the following risks except:
- a. Company risk
- b. Default risk
- c. Systemic risk
- d. Inflation risk

69. Tactically managing your portfolio according to the economic cycle is a strategy known as:
- a. Economic cycle rotation
- b. Strategic allocation
- c. Sector rotation
- d. Macro strategy

70. For an income investor in the 25% bracket, which of the following is subjected to the lowest federal income tax rate?
- a. Municipal bonds
- b. Treasury bonds
- c. Qualified dividends
- d. Bank CDs

71. An investor sells 1,000 shares of stock that he's held for two years for $11,500. He has received dividends of $200 over that time and his capital gain is $2,500, what is his cost basis?
- a. $8,800
- b. $9,000
- c. $9,200
- d. $9.00

10

72. The Alternative Minimum Tax is most likely to negatively impact:

a. C corporations that hold corporate owned life insurance (COLI)
b. Low tax retirees that own dividend paying stocks
c. A high income person with lots of tax deductions
d. A low tax bracket owner of municipal bond funds

73. What would be the tax consequences if a married couple gifted $23,000 worth of stock to their son in 2020 with a cost basis of $10,000 and he promptly sold it?

a. There would be gift tax and short term capital gains.
b. There would not be gift tax and short term capital gains.
c. There would be gift tax and long term capital gains.
d. There would not be gift tax and long term capital gains.

74. Which of the following actions does not exempt you from the 10% penalty for withdrawing from your IRA prior to age 59 ½?

a. Becoming permanently disabled
b. Using the withdrawal pay income taxes
c. Using the withdrawal for higher education expenses
d. Taking a series of equal periodic payments

75. For an employer looking to set up a retirement plan with flexibility being the most important priority, which would not be an acceptable choice?

a. A defined benefit plan
b. Profit sharing plan
c. 401k plan
d. SIMPLE IRA

76. Which retirement plan cannot be set up by an S corporation for its employees?

a. SEP IRA
b. Safe Harbor 401k
c. Keogh plan
d. ESOP plan

77. Which of the following is not considered a fiduciary for a pension plan?

a. An investment adviser to the plan
b. An individual exercising discretion on his own account
c. A member of the administrative committee
d. Officer of the corporation that selects members of the pension plan committee

78. Which of the following is not a requirement necessary to meet 404c testing for Safe Harbor status?

a. Diversified investment options
b. Financial and investment education
c. Access to a Certified Financial Planner for retirement planning advice
d. Access to investment prospectuses

79. Of the following duties, which is not an explicit duty of a plan fiduciary?

a. To diversify plan assets properly so as to minimize risk
b. To act in accordance with documents and instruments governing the plan
c. To not invest more than 40% of plan assets in equities
d. To act solely in the interest of the participants and plan beneficiaries

80. Which of the following characteristics is not true of 529 savings accounts?

a. Contributions are tax deductible
b. The beneficiary can be anyone
c. Withdrawals for qualified education expenses are federal tax free
d. Beneficiaries may be changed as long as they are related

81. Which account best meets the needs of a parent who wants to save for their child's college education, but doesn't want the child to have the money if they don't go to college?

a. A prepaid tuition account
b. A Coverdell educational savings account
c. An UTMA/UGMA account
d. A 529 college savings account

82. Which type of account is most likely to simply and inexpensively avoid probate?

a. Joint ownership with Rights of Survivorship
b. Pay-on-Death account
c. Joint ownership with Tenancy in Common
d. Single ownership with a beneficiary

83. Subscribing and paying a fee to an ECN allows you to what?

a. Display quotes and execute transactions
b. Trade securities after hours
c. To quote and trade anonymously
d. All of the above

84. Reg SHO requires broker-dealers to what?

a. Requires them to maintain proper margin for accounts involved in short selling
b. Requires them to locate and document that shares to be sold short exist
c. Requires them to allow shares to be sold short only after a downtick has occurred
d. Requires them to fine brokers that do not properly mark short sell orders

85. Which is not part of the basic information needed to execute a trade?

a. Bid
b. Offer
c. Last sale price
d. Current quote

86. In bond trading, the difference between the price an investor pays for a bond and the price the dealer paid is called what?

a. Commission
b. Markup
c. Spread
d. Margin

87. What type of order would be placed if the investor wanted to protect profits and wanted to sell the stock immediately if a certain price was hit?

a. Market order
b. Stop Market order
c. Stop Limit order
d. Limit order

88. Which is the most important metric to use when purchasing a bond for total return?

a. Current Yield
b. Yield to Maturity
c. Yield to Call
d. Taxable Equivalent Yield

89. For a retiree investor, the most important metric in evaluating an investment manager is:

a. Time-weighted return
b. Dollar-weighted return
c. Inflation adjusted return
d. Risk adjusted return

90. An investor in a 30% marginal federal tax bracket and a 7% state tax bracket would be better off buying:

a. A corporate bond yielding 5.2%
b. An out-of-state municipal bond yielding 4%
c. A Puerto Rico municipal bond yielding 3.5%
d. A US Treasury bond yielding 4.2%

91. Which of the following is NOT true of an Investment Advisor?

a. The majority of their income is from investment commissions
b. They are held to the fiduciary standard on their investment advice to clients
c. They must disclose exactly what services are included in fees they charge
d. They are usually compensated with fees rather than commissions

92. Which of the following is prohibited from registering with the SEC?

a. Adviser with $20 million assets under management
b. An Internet investment adviser
c. Adviser to a registered investment company
d. None of the above

93. Which of the following is not true concerning the Advisers Form ADV part 2?

a. It must include what services are provided and for what fees
b. It must be given to prospects 72 hours before a contract is signed
c. Education and business background of all officers of the firm
d. Criminal and regulatory disclosure over previous 10 years

94. Which of the following job duties does not necessitate the employee to become registered as an Investment Adviser Representative?

    a. Sells services of the firm
    b. Manages client accounts
    c. Manages graphic design and marketing materials
    d. Supervises employees

95. In which of the following situations does an Investment Adviser Representative have to register in the state where they do not have a place of business?

    a. Has only institutional clients in the state
    b. Has 10 institutional clients and 5 non-institutional clients in the state
    c. Has only 10 non-institutional clients in the state
    d. Has only 5 institutional and 5 non-institutional clients in the state

96. If an Investment Adviser Representative makes an investment recommendation based upon a research report prepared by another firm, the IAR must:

    a. Deliver the report on his Adviser's letterhead with his original commentary
    b. Disclose the conflict of using another firm's research
    c. Nothing as long as he doesn't pretend he wrote the report
    d. Determine if the other firm also owns the investment

97. An Investment Adviser Representative working for a federal covered advisor found to have violated the Investment Adviser's Act of 1940 is most likely to get in trouble with which agency?

    a. The Securities Exchange Commission (SEC)
    b. The State Administrator
    c. Financial Industry Regulatory Authority (FINRA)
    d. All of the above

98. Which of the following is true regarding the regulation of broker-dealers?

    a. They are covered by the Securities Exchange Act of 1934
    b. They are covered by the Investment Advisers Act of 1940
    c. They charge a percentage fee on the assets they manage
    d. They are a fiduciary for their clients

99. A broker dealer with a business in a state must register with that state administrator when?

    a. They have more than 5 institutional clients in that state
    b. They have more than 5 retail clients in that state
    c. They have more than 10 retail clients in that state
    d. All of the above

100. For which of the following activities must an agent of a broker dealer have proper written authorization?

    a. A broker deciding to wait an hour to get a better price on a stock purchase
    b. A broker waiting for an afternoon rally to sell a stock at a higher price that day
    c. A broker deciding to buy 100 or 200 shares depending on price
    d. All of the above

101. Which of the following is not a part of the post-registration "books and records" provisions that a broker-dealer is required to maintain?

a. Account documentation
b. Email correspondence
c. Birthday and Anniversary cards
d. None of the above

102. A person applying to work for a broker-dealer as an agent must disclose which of the following?

a. Financial condition and history
b. Criminal history
c. Qualifications and business history
d. All of the above

103. Which of the following is true regarding an agent of a broker dealer?

a. He or she is in the business of giving investment advice
b. He or she is in the business of effecting securities transactions for others
c. He or she is paid fees for investment advice
d. Assets under management is the key metric to determine his or her income

104. Which of the following needs to apply to be registered as an agent of a broker-dealer?

a. The new receptionist/office manager
b. Existing officer of broker-dealer
c. Existing passive investor in the broker-dealer
d. New sales supervisor

105. What are the net capital requirements for an agent of a broker-dealer?

a. $5,000
b. $10,000
c. A surety bond for $10,000
d. Zero

106. Which of the following is not a security?

a. Debenture
b. A futures contract
c. Option on a futures contract
d. A commodity futures contract

107. Which of the following is a security?

a. Universal life insurance contract
b. Single stock futures contract
c. Fixed annuity
d. Endowment policy

108. Which of the following is not true regarding the state registration of a security?

a. Registrations are effective for one year
b. Registration statement must include consent to service of process
c. Only the issuer is allowed to file for registration of a security
d. Not all securities must be registered with the state

109. A state administrator may require a federal covered security to register by notice filing and provide which of the following?

a. All documents filed with their registration statements filed with the SEC
b. Filing fees
c. A consent to service of process
d. All of the above

110. Which of the following does not fall under the state administrator's authority according to the Uniform Securities Act?

a. A federal covered security not registered with the state
b. A fixed annuity
c. A security registered with both the SEC and the state
d. A variable universal life insurance policy

111. Which of the following administrative orders is considered a non-punitive order?

a. Suspension of license
b. Revocation of license
c. Cease and desist order
d. Withdrawal of license

112. In order to provide necessary protection to investors, a state administrator may do all of the following except:

a. Issue subpoenas
b. Issue legal injunctions to prevent illegal activity
c. Administer oaths and take testimony
d. Investigate as necessary both inside and outside the state

113. Civil liabilities that may be sought by investors under the Uniform Securities Act include all of the following except:

a. Money paid for investment advice
b. Court costs and attorneys' fees
c. Any profits the adviser made from investors' money
d. Price paid for security plus interest

114. Which of the following communications with clients and prospects need to be kept on file?

a. Thank you notes
b. Trade confirmations
c. Birthday cards
d. All of the above

115. In which case it is appropriate for an Investment Adviser to offer clients a performance guarantee?

a. Never
b. Only when explaining life insurance guarantees
c. Only when explaining US Treasury bonds
d. Only when explaining annuity guarantees

16

116. Which of the following representations is an Investment Adviser Representative not permitted to use, even if he actually earned it?

    a. Chartered Financial Analyst
    b. Certified Financial Planner
    c. Certified Financial Gerontologist
    d. Accredited Wealth Management Advisor

117. Which of the following disclosures must be made on the Form ADV part 2 and delivered to prospects and clients?

    a. What mutual funds are typically recommended
    b. How much money the Investment Adviser makes from 12b 1 fees
    c. Criminal disclosure over past 10 years
    d. What the investment performance was of their average client over the past 12 months

118. Which of the following types of compensation does not need to be disclosed to prospects and clients?

    a. Fees charged for services
    b. Soft dollars for placing trades through particular broker-dealers
    c. Commissions earned on products
    d. None of the above

119. Which methods of compensation are not allowed for an agent of a broker dealer?

    a. Mutual fund 12b-1 fees
    b. Markups on bonds
    c. Performance based fees
    d. Commissions on annuities

120. What is the most common method for a Registered Investment Advisor to be paid for advice?

    a. Commissions on sales of securities
    b. Commissions on sales of insurance
    c. Fees based on a percentage of assets under management
    d. A blend of commissions and fees on securities

121. "Wrap accounts" have a benefit of eliminating the potential for what abuse?

    a. Fraud
    b. Churning
    c. Advisers not disclosing soft dollar commissions
    d. Commingling of funds

122. Which standard of care is most important for an Investment Adviser?

    a. As long as the client does not lose money on an investment
    b. As long as the investment is "suitable"
    c. As long as the advice is what a "prudent" man would do
    d. All of the above

123. An adviser with trading authorization over an account, but not custody of that account, must maintain what minimum net capital?

a. Zero
b. A Surety bond for $10,000
c. $10,000
d. $35,000

124. An Investment Adviser having discretion over his clients' portfolios is considered:

a. A portfolio manager
b. A Fiduciary
c. A financial planner
d. All of the above

125. Which of the following activities would not coincide with proper behavior under the Prudent Investor Standards?

a. Maintaining proper asset diversification
b. Doing due diligence on investments
c. Commingling of accounts for commission discounts
d. Outsourcing of investment decisions on a portion of the assets

126. In which of the following situations is it permissible for an Adviser to receive a loan from a client?

a. When the amount is under $20,000
b. When the client is a relative
c. When the client is a banker operating in his professional capacity
d. When the duration of the loan is less than 30 days

127. Which of the following soft-dollar methods of compensation are not allowable to an Investment Adviser?

a. Trade processing services
b. Research reports
c. Software to aid in research
d. Cell phone to conduct business out of the office

128. Which is not an important issue the NASAA will look at when reviewing Investment Advisers that have custody over client assets?

a. Are clients getting monthly account statements?
b. Is there evidence of excessive trading in the account?
c. Are the assets maintained in segregated accounts?
d. Does the Form ADV reflect the fact that the IA has custody?

129. When an Investment Adviser Representative offers a client an investment opportunity in a security not sponsored by the firm, this is known as:

a. Alternative investments
b. Selling away
c. All of the above
d. None of the above

130. The most serious penalty that might be given for insider trading under the Insider Trading and Securities Fraud Enforcement Act is:

    a. Civil penalty up to 100% of profit
    b. Revocation of license and civil penalty of 200% of profits
    c. Years in federal prison and civil penalties of many times the profit
    d. Liability of up to 100% of what "contemporaneous traders" can prove injury

Answers and Explanations

1. C: Inflation. Over time, inflationary forces cause prices to increase, thereby causing the value of what a "dollar" will buy to decrease. For example, movie theater tickets have risen consistently over time so that the same movie experience can now cost 3x what it did twenty years ago.

2. B: The CPI, or Consumer Price Index. Food and energy prices are usually stripped out because of their volatility to give a "core" inflation rate.

3. C: The S&P 500 is by far the most widely followed leading economic indicator. While unemployment claims and consumer confidence are also leading indicators, they are used in conjunction with the stock markets. The payroll numbers are a coincident indicator.

4. B: A recession. A recession is defined as two consecutive quarters of declining GDP, up to six. Any more than six consecutive is a Depression.

5. C: CPI data is lagging. M2 and new building permits are leading indicators and personal income levels is considered a coincident indicator.

6. C: The situation of short term rates being higher than longer term rates is not normal, and is therefore inverted. This is often a predictor of negative economic growth and is viewed by some as a recession indicator.

7. C: The Current ratio incorporates inventory as well as current assets and liabilities

8. D: Another name for the operating margin is EBIT, or Earnings Before Interest and Taxes. So interest and tax expenses are not figured into the operating margin.

9. C: Saleable assets would be included in inventory which is a current asset.

10. D: The 10-Q is quarterly, the 10-K is annual, and the 8-K is for news filed before the next 10-Q or 10-K.

11. D: The "price" is often the change factor for the PE ratio and therefore the ratio is a good measure of the value of a stock to investors

12. B: NPV is relevant when calculating future cash flows and whether the cost of current investment will be returned in future increased cash flows or not.

13. C: When numbers are added up and then divided to get the "average", that is the Mean.

14. A: Standard deviation is the normal variation of the investment- or ride- going both up and down.

15. A: Market risk is systematic, which cannot be diversified away through geographic, asset class or country diversification.

16. A: Purchasing power, or inflation, is still a risk for investors in zero coupon bonds.

17. B: Opportunity cost is the 1% given up in hopes of higher returns.

18. C: Although knowing what you invest in is great, limiting investments to one industry leaves you very vulnerable to multiple risks.

19. A: Common stockholders are at the end of the line in a liquidation scenario, often receiving nothing at all after more senior parties are paid.

20. C: Money market securities are 12 months or less, with the majority maturing in six months or less. Usually they are issued at a discount.

21. A: You can lose money in a brokered CD, typically if you need to access the cash prior to maturity and the market is not very liquid. You can generally get higher yields, get access to principal prior to maturity- at a cost- and easily have multiple CDs fully insured for 250k each without opening multiple accounts at different banks.

22. D: Bran is something most often found in cereal. TAN, RAN, TRAN, and BAN are varieties of municipal notes backed by taxes, revenues, taxes and revenues, and bonds.

23. D: A double-barreled bond is one that is backed by both GO taxing authority as well as revenues from a particular project.

24. B: Ginnie Mae, as it's commonly known, is the only agency directly backed by the government, the others being "government sponsored".

25. C: Brady bonds are issued by emerging market countries, but are collateralized by US Treasury securities, reducing much of the risk typical with EM bonds.

26. D: A convertible bond will always be priced relative to the stock

27. B: HH bonds are no longer being issued by the US Treasury as of September 1, 2004.

28. C: For Premium bonds, the stated coupon yield is highest, then the current yield, then the yield to maturity

29. D: The coupon rate is the interest rate paid at par, or the nominal yield, which does not take into account the bond trading at a premium or a discount, which would be the current yield.

30. B: Long term bonds are the most vulnerable to rising interest rates. REITs and stocks fare the best in a rising rate environment and the shorter duration of short term bonds get hurt much less than long term bonds.

31. B: Restricted shares are a classification of issued shares, while authorized shares are the largest allowable number of shares that can be issued by a company.

32. D: There is no such thing as the dividend date. First comes the declaration date, then the record date, then the payable date.

33. C: While most preferreds are considered to pay in "perpetuity", there is not actually a perpetual preferred.

34. A: Warrants are the longest term security that allow you to purchase a stock at a given price

35. C: ADRs do have currency risk, are not denominated in USD, and are not issued in the US. The receipt is issued to someone in the US for a foreign stock held on deposit in another country.

36. C: The PEG (Price-to-Earnings Growth) ratio. This calculation helps growth investors assess the price of a stock in relation to its expected growth rate.

37. C: Value investors are typically most interested in buying a company at or below its intrinsic value

38. D: Using a letter of intent to achieve a higher level of breakpoint discount is the best way. Typically, the money needs to be invested over the next 13 months.

39. C: Demographics applies to people, not stocks.

40. C: Private Equity funds are not regulated by the 1940 Act, but are limited to only "Accredited investors", those with substantial assets and an assumed higher level of knowledge and sophistication.

41. C: ETFs are traded just like a stock and have constant and instant liquidity, whereas UITs do not.

42. C: Closed-ends trade like stocks on the open market and can trade above or below the NAV.

43. B: The NAV (Net asset value) is the cheapest price at which you can buy an open-end mutual fund. The POP is with no discount, and the ROA and LOI allow discounts.

44. D: Both selling a call option and buying a put will allow you to make money by a stock price declining.

45. D: All of the above are standard for most hedge funds.

46. B: PE funds are structured as limited partnerships, and are only for accredited investors and typically do have long lockup periods.

47. A: Term insurance is only insurance, with no savings built into it.

48. C: The immediate annuity is most likely the best option for someone who needs income now.

49. B: VUL is best, as it provides life insurance and also has a savings and investment component using mutual funds.

50. D: A fixed annuity is best for someone very risk averse and without a long time horizon for investing.

51. C: The sole proprietorship offers the owner no additional liability protection, unlike all three other business structures.

52. C: The LLC gives the best liability protection and avoids double taxation.

53. D: The C corporation is the best structure to attract investment capital

54. A: In an LLP, the General partner has a fiduciary relationship to the limited partners

55. B: Except in extreme cases, a client's individual health issues don't really factor in to his or her profile.

Mometrix

56. C: The investor's time horizon is clearly the most important information in developing his or her ability to take risk with their investments.

57. D: Municipal bonds should be considered for someone in a high tax bracket that is nearing retirement.

58. C: With a low risk tolerance and a short time horizon, individual small caps should be eliminated from consideration.

59. C: Portfolio optimization is about putting together different investments with differing risk/reward characteristics into a portfolio that overall achieves the highest return with the least risk. Modern portfolio theory is all about managing the multiple investments to create an overall portfolio that best reflects the needs of the investor.

60. A: The Weak form says that all past stock prices are reflected in today's price. However, fundamental analysis can be used to identify stocks that are currently over or undervalued.

61. D: The Capital Asset Pricing Model uses the risk free rate of return to calculate the expected return of an investment that tries to take in the risk of an investment. The goal is to only make investments where the expected return is worth the increased risk over the "risk-free" rate of return available.

62. B: Strategic asset allocation is the investment strategy most appropriate for a believer in the strong form of the Efficient Market Hypothesis. Strategies such as sector rotation and tactical asset allocation are incompatible with the strong form as they suggest outperformance can be gained through these strategies.

63. D: Buy and hold is style agnostic, it could be with growth or value stocks, or mutual funds or exchange traded funds. This approach exclusively focuses on the long term returns of an investment and "holds" through all the ups and downs of the intervening years.

64. C: The dividend payout ratio is important for evaluating the stability and security of a stock's dividend. An income investor is looking for the dividend as the most important part of the investment, so knowing the security of that dividend going forward is preeminent.

65. A: While some of the others may be true, we cannot say they are for certain. The only thing we know for certain is that it is a diversified portfolio.

66. C: Rebalancing as a discipline helps to ensure the investor sells high and buys low. It also helps to maintain proper diversification and strategic asset allocation.

67. B: Dollar cost averaging, putting in equal amounts on a regular (monthly, for ex.) basis allows more shares to be bought when prices are lower and less when prices are higher. Over time, this allows the overall cost basis to be lower and therefore the potential to be higher. It also reduces the psychological fear of when to make an investment.

68. C: Systemic risk cannot be reduced by diversifying your investments within the system. If the system crashes, all investments contained in that system are vulnerable.

69. C: Sector rotation is a fundamental strategy using the cycles of the economy to determine which sectors of the economy should be performing the best during a given cycle. Attempting to be in the stocks in those sectors and rotating out of the sectors out of sync with the economic cycle is a strategy that can use technicals to help identify timing, but it is fundamentally based.

70. A: Municipal bonds are exempt from federal income tax, and both Treasury bonds and CD's are taxable at your individual tax bracket. Qualified dividends are taxed at 15%.

71. B: $9,000 is his cost basis. 9,000 plus 2,500 is 11,500. In this case, the number of shares or share price is irrelevant, and the dividends were not reinvested so they don't impact the cost basis but were taxed as income when received.

72. C: The primary trigger for the Alternative Minimum Tax is being in an upper income tax bracket. The real bite of the AMT is that many of the normal deductions are not allowed, which greatly increases the tax bill of your normal upper bracket filer.

73. D: Individuals are allowed to give up to $15,000 gift tax free (2020), so no gift taxes. As a gift, he would inherit his parents' cost basis as well as holding period, so there would be long term capital gains.

74. B: Taking money from your IRA to pay income taxes does not avoid the 10% penalty. It's actually a truly terrible idea because that money would be taxed at ordinary income tax rates, and the 10% penalty would be incurred on top of that.

75. A: A defined benefit plan would be the least flexible plan, as the contributions are determined by the future benefit mandated and do not allow any flexibility as to when and how much the contributions are.

76. C: Keogh plans may only be set up for sole proprietorship companies, and contributions are allowed as a % of self-employment income.

77. B: An individual that exercises discretion over his or her own account is not a fiduciary, but if he or she exercises discretion over any part of the plan, this individual would be considered a fiduciary.

78. C: There is a plethora of requirements of the plan sponsor in order to meet safe harbor status, principally involving investment options, disclosures, and education. However, having access to a CFP professional is not one of them.

79. C: There is no specific prohibition on investment allocations except as laid out in the plan specific Investment Policy Statement.

80. A: 529 contributions are made with after tax money, although some states may offer various incentives for their state specific plans, there are no federal tax breaks for 529 contributions.

81. D: A 529 remains the property of the owner of the account growing tax deferred until the money is withdrawn. If the beneficiary does not use the money for education, the owner may pay taxes and use the money for whatever they choose.

82. B: The pay-on-death account is designed to avoid probate and be transferred directly to beneficiary upon the death of the account owner.

83. D: Subscribing by paying a fee to an ECN, such as Instinet or NYSE ARCA, allows you to trade after hours, trade anonymously, and allows you to display quotes and execute transactions directly.

84. B: Reg SHO requires broker-dealers to locate and document shares available to be sold short and reasonably believe the shares can be delivered (T + 3) as well as making sure all orders are properly marked. BD's are not required to fine brokers, but may be fined themselves.

85. C: While useful to know, it is not really relevant to executing a trade. There will be times when the last sale price is miles away from the current bid/offer spread.

86. C: The spread is the difference the dealer makes between what it pays for a bond and what it then sells a bond for. The commission will come out of that spread.

87. B: A stop market order is triggered when a certain price is hit and then it turns into a market order and is sold at the next market price. A stop limit is triggered the same, but then becomes a price specific limit order.

88. B: Yield to maturity is the most relevant metric to use for investing in bonds for total return. The others may not apply to a particular bond at all.

89. D: The amount of return for risk taken is the single most important metric for most investors, but especially for investors who are retired and have to rely on the money they've saved to last the rest of their lives.

90. B: Corporate bonds are not tax-exempt, out-of-state muni bonds are exempt from federal income taxes but usually not state income taxes, Puerto Rico muni bonds are exempt from all levels of income tax, and US Treasury bonds are exempt solely from federal income tax. Hence the corporate bond's TEY is 5.2%, the out-of-state bond's TEY = 4% / (1 – 30%) = 5.71%, the Puerto Rico bond's TEY = 3.5% / (1 – 30% - 7%) = 5.56%, and the Treasury bond's TEY = 4.2% / (1 – 7%) = 4.52%. The out-of-state bond has the highest tax-equivalent yield (TEY).

Puerto Rico bonds are local, state, and federal tax free. The TEY is 5.55% better than the other alternatives after taxation is considered.

91. A: An Investment Adviser operates under a fiduciary relationship, usually managing money on behalf of clients and is not in the business of selling products. They usually charge fees based on Assets Under Management.

92. A: Per the Dodd-Frank Act, which aimed to increase state oversight in securities markets, all small investment advisers – defined as those advisers with under $25 million in managed assets – are required to register with their state (unless they're in Wyoming) and prohibited, not merely exempted, from registering with the SEC.

93. B: The Form ADV part 2 must be given to prospects and clients within 48 hours before signing a contract. Alternatively, it can be given at the time of signing a contract as long as they have 5 days in which they may cancel without penalty.

94. C: Graphic design and marketing work is not something that requires the employee to be registered as an IAR.

95. C: The key is whether or not the IAR has more than 5 NON- Institutional clients in a state. If so, they must register, if they only have institutional clients in the state they are not required to register.

96. C: Nothing needs be done. The only problem occurs if the IAR is trying to pass off someone else's research as his own.

97. D: An IAR is liable to be in trouble with the state administrator for engaging in any conduct that is a violation of the securities laws of the state regardless of whether or not they are registered with the state or the SEC. Anything warranting action from the SEC and the state administrator will bring additional action from FINRA.

98. A: Broker-dealers are covered by the Securities Act of 1934, and charge a commission on transactions rather than a percentage fee of assets. Broker-dealers operate under the suitability rule rather than as fiduciaries.

99. D: A broker-dealer must register in every state where they have a place of business, regardless of how many or what kind of customers they have in that state.

100. C: An agent of a broker dealer must have written authorization for anything beyond same day time/price discretion. Changing the number of shares is way beyond simple time/price discretion.

101. D: All of these and much more are required to be kept on file and accessible to regulators, all documentation, communication, sales and marketing material, and nearly everything else that might be used in dealing with a broker-dealer's customers.

102. D: All of the above must be disclosed, along with educational background, any prior customer complaints and anything at all to do with rule-breaking in the financial industry.

103. B: An Investment adviser, or an IAR, is in the business of giving investment advice. Agents of broker-dealers are simply in the business of effecting "suitable" transactions of securities for others.

104. D: Existing employees are considered to already be registered with an active registered broker-dealer. Anyone supervising agents involved in sales activities must be registered.

105. D: There are no net capital requirements for an agent, but there are requirements for the broker-dealer itself.

106. D: Futures contracts are securities, but a commodity futures contract is not a security.

107. B: Most insurance contracts, other than a variable universal policy, are not securities. A commodity futures contract is the only futures contract that is not a security.

108. C: Underwriters may file the registration on behalf of the issuer. Many securities do not have to be registered at the state level.

109. D: Registration by notification with states is mostly an opportunity to collect filing fees for the states. They may require all of the above documents.

110. B: A fixed annuity is not a security, so therefore it does not fall under the Uniform Securities Act at all.

111. D: A withdrawal order is simply an order responding to a request for a withdrawal of a license. It is not punitive in nature, as the withdrawal is not a penalty.

112. B: An administrator may issue a cease and desist order, but only a court of law may issue a legal injunction.

113. C: Profits the adviser may have made from investing money is not recoverable. Price paid for security, plus interest, anything paid for advice, plus attorney's fees and court costs, MINUS any income received on the security investment may all be sued for and recovered.

114. D: All communications with clients and prospects, whether securities-related or not, need to be kept on file.

115. A: Never. Explaining guarantees offered by an insurance or annuity company, or FDIC guarantees is fine, but that is completely separate from the Adviser offering those guarantees.

116. C: Many of the "senior" type of designations out there are looked upon very skeptically by regulators. The other designations are governed by the boards responsible for issuing those designations.

117. C: Any criminal and regulatory issues from the past 10 years must be disclosed on the Form ADV part 2. While individual mutual funds do not need to be named, the IA must disclose the types of securities about which advice will be rendered.

118. D: Especially in the area of compensation, any way that you possibly get paid from, or because of, clients needs to be disclosed.

119. C: An agent of a broker dealer is not allowed to be paid through a performance fee arrangement

120. C: Fees paid to the RIA based on a percentage of assets under management is the most common way for Advisers to get paid. Many fee-only advisers will outsource insurance and other products instead of take commissions.

121. B: Because the fees for advice and brokerage commissions are "wrapped" into one account, the potential for churning is eliminated. All trades are done by the portfolio manager because he/she believes it to be a good investment, not as a way to increase his/her income through commissions.

122. C: Advisers are not held to the "suitability" standard, but to the much higher fiduciary standard. They can easily run afoul of the Prudent investor standards while only purchasing "suitable" securities. And they can be in trouble even if the investment makes a profit.

123. C: Advisers with custody must maintain $35,000 in minimum net capital, but if they only have discretion and not custody, they are only required to maintain $10,000.

124. B: An adviser managing money for clients for a fee is a fiduciary. This determines the legal standard to which they are held. Portfolio manager and financial planner are different terms that describe jobs and may or may not be fiduciaries.

125. C: Commingling of accounts is never a good idea. Even in view of trying to save money for the accounts, you're likely to have broken some basic management rules of keeping fiduciary accounts strictly segregated.

126. C: There are allowances for taking a loan from a client such as a banker or mortgage broker when they are acting in their professional capacity, because in that case, the loan is not actually coming from the client personally.

127. D: Cell phones are on the list of non-allowable forms of soft-dollar compensation, no matter how the business need is rationalized.

128. A: The NASAA will look that clients receive itemized account statements at least every three months showing the assets and the activity in the account. Monthly statements are not required, although that is the norm.

129. D: Selling away is a violation that occurs when an agent, or a registered representative, NOT an IAR, offers an investment opportunity not sponsored by the firm. Usually this is followed by immediate dismissal from the firm.

130. C: Insider trading is liable to land you in federal prison on a criminal conviction and will probably also result in a fine of several times the amount of profits; opens up liability to contemporaneous traders; and is guaranteed to result in the loss of registration and the prohibition of future work in the financial industry.

Practice Test #2

1. A value investor would likely try to purchase cyclical stocks at what point in the business cycle?

    a. The Expansion phase
    b. The Peak phase
    c. The Contraction phase
    d. The Trough phase

2. An investor should go to defensive stocks at what point of the business cycle?

    a. The Expansion phase
    b. The Peak phase
    c. The Contraction phase
    d. The Trough phase

3. Monetary policy tools, used by the Federal Reserve, primarily are:

    a. The reserve requirement
    b. Open Market operations
    c. The discount rate
    d. All of the above

4. All of the following are factors of a country's balance of trade except:

    a. Trade surplus
    b. Trade deficit
    c. Current account
    d. Balance of payments

5. Which of the following is most directly correlated to a country's currency strength or weakness?

    a. Interest rates
    b. Balance of trade
    c. The business cycle
    d. Gross domestic product

6. The difference in yields between the 10-yr Treasury and high yield "junk" bonds is the yield spread, also called the "risk premium". When the spread widens, it is an indicator of which of the following?

    1. Investor confidence in the economy
    2. Investor fears for the economy
    3. Investor preference for stocks over bonds
    4. Investor preference for safer investments

    a. 1 and 3
    b. 2 and 4
    c. 1 and 4
    d. 2 and 3

7. On a balance sheet, which of the following would not be considered a current liability?

a. Employees payroll
b. SBA loan
c. Bills for inventory
d. Social Security taxes for employees

8. On an income statement, all of the following would be factored into the gross margin except which of the following?

a. Operating expenses
b. Cost of goods sold
c. Sales revenue
d. Packaging

9. Stockholders' equity can be defined as:

1. Assets - Liabilities
2. Net worth
3. Operating profits
4. Par value of common stock

a. 1 and 2
b. 3 and 4
c. 1, 2, and 3
d. All of the above

10. Which of the following metrics give you an idea of whether or not a stock is expensive or cheap?

a. Gross margin
b. Price to earnings multiple
c. Dividend payout ratio
d. Earnings before Interest, Taxes, Depreciation, and Amortization

11. Which of the following financial metrics will not be found in a company's 10-K?

a. Capital Expenditures
b. Changes in operating margins
c. Changes in price to earnings ratio
d. S, G, and A expenses

12. Which of the following mutual funds would you most like to invest in?

a. The one with the highest standard deviation
b. The one with the highest Sharpe ratio
c. The one with the highest Sortino ratio
d. The one with the highest positive Alpha

13. If someone offered you $100,000 today, or $120,000 five years from now, you would need to calculate what in order to make a good decision?

a. The time value of money
b. The internal rate of return (IRR)
c. The future value
d. The net present value (NPV)

14. In a classroom of kids, 2 kids are 3'4" tall, 2 kids are 3'6" tall, 2 kids are 4' tall, 2 kids are 4'3" tall, and 2 kids are 4'8" tall. What is the median height?

    a. 3'11"
    b. 4'0"
    c. 4'1"
    d. 3'9"

15. Forsaking a guaranteed return of 3% in order to pursue a 10% return is known as what?

    a. Inflation risk
    b. Greener grass principle
    c. Opportunity cost
    d. Market risk

16. A retiree today heavily invested in fixed income faces which of the following risks?

    a. Interest rate risk
    b. Credit risk
    c. Purchasing power risk
    d. All of the above

17. Which of the following is not a good way to diversify non-systematic risk in a portfolio?

    a. Using ETFs instead of individual stocks
    b. Investing in multiple countries
    c. Buy deep value equities
    d. Using mutual funds instead of individual stocks

18. One of the most overlooked risks by conservative investors is:

    a. Default risk
    b. Liquidity risk
    c. Currency risk
    d. Purchasing power risk

19. Emerging markets equity investors generally don't have to worry about which of the following risks?

    a. Reinvestment risk
    b. Political risk
    c. Currency risk
    d. Opportunity cost

20. What kind of money market security is most often used for international business transactions?

    a. Repurchase agreements
    b. US T-bills
    c. Banker's Acceptance
    d. Reverse repurchase agreements

21. Which money market instrument doesn't really have a secondary, liquid market?

a. Commercial paper
b. Repurchase agreements
c. Bankers Acceptance
d. T-bills

22. Which money market instrument would normally pay a lower interest rate than others of similar maturity?

a. Commercial paper
b. T-bills
c. CDs
d. Tax exempt municipal notes

23. Which of the following is not a reason for investing in US Government bonds?

a. Safety
b. High interest rates
c. Local and state tax treatment
d. Liquidity

24. Which of the following bonds does not have a secondary market?

a. TIPS
b. T-bills
c. I Bonds
d. Zero coupon bonds

25. If a bond, convertible into common at a 25:1 ratio, is trading at $1,250 and the stock price is $50, you would say the bond is:

a. At parity
b. At a premium
c. At a discount
d. At equivalency

26. In which of the following interest rate environments are bonds most likely to be called?

a. In a rising rate environment
b. In a falling rate environment
c. In a steady interest rate environment
d. The interest rate environment is not relevant

27. Which of the following can you avoid by investing in international Eurodollar bonds?

a. Reinvestment risk
b. Political risk
c. Currency risk
d. Inflation risk

28. For a holder of a discount bond, which of the following will not be moved by a change in interest rates?

    a. Yield to maturity
    b. Yield to call
    c. Nominal yield
    d. Current yield

29. A bond rating from Moody's of Baa is equal to:

    a. S&P A
    b. Fitch's BBB
    c. S&P A
    d. Fitch's BB

30. If a convertible bond is convertible at 40:1, and the bond is trading at $1,150, what is the stock's price?

    a. $29.25
    b. $28.75
    c. $28.25
    d. $25

31. The best way for an American investor to get exposure to foreign stocks:

    a. Warrants
    b. REITs
    c. ADRs
    d. Preferred stocks

32. Which is not a benefit of investing in Preferred stock over common stock?

    a. Senior position in a liquidation event
    b. Senior position in dividend payments
    c. Greater chance for capital gains
    d. Don't have to bother with voting rights issues

33. What is the total return for a stock that was bought at $45.50, and is now at $54.25 and paid dividends of $2.50?

    a. 19.2%
    b. 23%
    c. 24.7%
    d. 27.5%

34. Using the Rule of 72, which of the following investments would double in 14 years?

    a. A preferred stock paying 6%
    b. A corporate bond paying 7%
    c. A municipal bond paying 5%
    d. A common stock paying 2% dividend and growing by 5%

35. The best option for someone wanting to invest in real estate, but needing liquidity, is:

a. REITs
b. Preferred stock in a real estate company
c. Common stock in a real estate company
d. ADRs

36. All of the following are fundamental ways to value a stock, except:

a. Price to Earnings ratio
b. Market Capitalization
c. Price to Book ratio
d. Price to Sales ratio

37. Which combination of factors is most likely to be used by fundamental investors?

1. 200 day moving average
2. Advance/Decline ratio
3. Price/Sales ratio
4. Price/Earnings ratio

a. 1 and 2
b. 2 and 3
c. 3 and 4
d. 2 and 4

38. The primary benefit of a pooled investment is:

a. Diversification
b. Professional management
c. Better performance
d. Reduced expenses

39. Which of the following is not a type of mutual fund?

a. A Balanced fund
b. A Long/Short fund
c. An Equity Income fund
d. A Growth fund

40. Typically, which of the following will have the lowest operating expenses?

a. Closed end mutual fund
b. Unit Investment trust
c. REIT
d. An Exchange traded fund

41. For a long term individual investor, which share class of a regular open end mutual fund will be cheapest?

a. A shares
b. B shares
c. C shares
d. R shares

42. Which of the following can be purchased at a significant discount to its NAV?

a. An open end mutual fund
b. A closed-end mutual fund
c. An ETF
d. A UIT

43. One primary advantage of reinvesting mutual fund dividends is:

a. Dividends are not taxed when reinvested
b. The sales charge is reduced
c. Additional shares are purchased at NAV
d. There is no advantage

44. The primary difference between an option and a forward contract is:

a. The length of time covered by the contract
b. The cost of the contract
c. Forwards are contracts on commodities while options are on stocks
d. Options are transferable while forwards are not

45. Hedge funds are able to utilize what investment options that mutual funds are not?

a. Short selling
b. Concentrated positions
c. Sophisticated options strategies
d. All of the above

46. What is one of the benefits of a hedge fund of funds?

a. Diversification
b. Less risk
c. Higher returns
d. Lower fees

47. What type of insurance policy is the least expensive?

a. Whole life
b. Term life
c. Universal life
d. Variable life

48. What type of annuity is probably best suited for an investor who is only comfortable with CD's?

a. An equity-indexed annuity
b. A variable annuity
c. An immediate annuity
d. A fixed annuity

49. What type of annuity might be best suited for a young, conservative investor?

a. A fixed annuity
b. A variable annuity
c. An equity indexed annuity
d. An immediate annuity

50. What risk are variable annuities particularly suited to address?

a. Systematic risk
b. Inflation risk
c. Interest rate risk
d. The risk of outliving your savings

51. What is the simplest, easiest, and cheapest form of business to start?

a. Sole proprietorship
b. LLP
c. LLC
d. General partnership

52. What is the biggest downside to running a sole proprietorship?

a. Taxation
b. Dealing with limited partners
c. Liability
d. Limits on numbers of shareholders

53. What business structure is limited to only 100 shareholders?

a. LLP
b. LLC
c. C corp
d. S corp

54. What is the least advantageous structure when it comes to taxation?

a. Sole proprietorship
b. LLP
c. LLC
d. C corp

55. For a 29-year-old single client, with a high risk tolerance, low tax bracket, and $50,000 in savings, we can eliminate what asset class from our recommendation?

a. Money market funds
b. Municipal bond funds
c. Emerging market stock funds
d. Individual dividend paying stocks

56. Of the following data, what point is not necessary when developing a client's profile and objectives?

a. Discretionary income
b. Job description
c. Existing assets
d. Time horizon

57. Which of the following would not be advisable for someone with a low risk tolerance and a high need for liquidity?

a. Money market funds
b. A short term bond fund
c. A fixed annuity
d. A short term bond ETF

58. What is the monthly discretionary income of a client with $8,000 of salary, $500 of investment income and expenses of $2,000 taxes, $4,000 living expenses, and $500 of travel and entertainment expenses?

a. $8,000
b. $2,500
c. $2,000
d. $1,500

59. The "efficient frontier" is most closely associated with what?

a. The efficient market hypothesis
b. The CAPM
c. Asset allocation
d. Modern portfolio theory

60. A Random Walk Down Wall Street by Burton Malkiel spotlighted what?

a. Modern Portfolio theory
b. The efficient market hypothesis
c. The capital asset pricing model
d. The efficient frontier

61. A risk free rate of return is used in which of the following?

a. Capital asset pricing model
b. Strong form of efficient market hypothesis
c. Weak form of efficient market hypothesis
d. Modern portfolio theory

62. Facets of strategic asset allocation involve all of the following except:

a. Asset class diversification
b. Sector diversification
c. Enhanced indexing
d. Style diversification

63. Which of the following factors do not impact one's decision to choose active over passive management?

a. Cheaper costs of index funds
b. Long-term capital gains tax rates
c. Believing in the efficiency of markets
d. Believing managers are not smarter than the markets

64. Tactical asset allocation differs from Strategic asset allocation in which of the following way?

a. Tactical is more active
b. Tactical is more tax efficient
c. Strategic is more technically oriented
d. Strategic is more tax efficient

65. A value investor is more inclined to believe in:

a. Efficient market hypothesis
b. Buy and hold methods
c. Dollar cost averaging
d. Intrinsic value

66. Someone who diversifies across sectors, asset classes, styles and then meticulously rebalances every 12 months is said to be practicing:

a. Strategic asset allocation
b. Tactical asset allocation
c. Sector rotation
d. Dollar cost averaging

67. An investor who believes in the efficient market hypothesis would invest in which of the following?

a. Actively managed mutual fund
b. Long / short hedge fund
c. An investment newsletter
d. An indexed mutual fund

68. Regularly investing money into a mutual fund on a monthly basis is an example of:

a. Buy and hold investing
b. Dollar cost averaging
c. Passive investing
d. Diversification

69. Investing 90% of your assets in the company stock of your employer is not a good example of what?

a. Dollar cost averaging
b. Buy and hold investing
c. Diversification
d. Tactical asset allocation

70. If an individual is in the lowest tax bracket, which of the following has the lowest rate?

a. Capital gains
b. Preferred stock dividends
c. REIT dividends
d. Qualified dividends

71. For individuals in the 15% tax bracket, what is the long term capital gains rate for 2013?

   a. 0%
   b. 10%
   c. 15%
   d. 20%

72. "Double taxation" refers to which of the following?

   a. Paying taxes on dividends from a company that already paid corporate taxes
   b. The fact that many married couples pay more in tax than they would if they were single
   c. When you double your money in capital gains, but then have to pay taxes on the gain
   d. The fact that those in the top tax bracket pay twice what the average American pays

73. An investor buys 100 shares of stock for $20,000, but the stock goes down to $175 and she sells it for a short term loss. However, she still really likes the stock so a few weeks later she buys 120 shares planning to hold them for many years. The tax situation is as follows.

   a. She has a short term capital loss of $2,500
   b. She can offset her long term gain with the short term loss
   c. She can use the loss to offset her income
   d. She has triggered "wash sale" rules and there is no tax loss

74. Which retirement plan is best if you're looking for a tax deduction?

   a. Roth IRA
   b. Traditional IRA
   c. 401k
   d. 403b

75. The biggest advantage of a Roth IRA is:

   a. Tax deferral of gains
   b. Tax deductibility of contribution
   c. Tax free withdrawals
   d. Cheaper investment options through group plan

76. Which qualified plan would be best for an older worker who needs to save rapidly for retirement?

   a. A 401k with profit sharing
   b. A defined benefit pension plan
   c. A SEP IRA
   d. An ESOP

77. Which of the following would not be a fiduciary of a pension plan?

   a. The CEO of the company
   b. Trustee of the plan
   c. Investment advisers hired to manage the money
   d. Investment committee members

78. Which of the following is not a requirement to meet Safe Harbor requirements?

a. Provide solid recommendations of good investments in the plan
b. Provide sufficient education and information about the plan
c. Provide the ability to change investment allocations at least quarterly
d. Offer at least three choices with materially different risk and return characteristics

79. When is it acceptable to override the Investment Policy Statement?

a. When a fund has expanded or contracted by more than 40%
b. When requested by a majority of plan participants
c. Only when it is clearly prudent to do so
d. Only to avoid the risk of large losses

80. What type of account is exclusively for higher education costs?

a. UTMA
b. Coverdell
c. 529
d. Keogh

81. Which of the following can you not purchase on margin inside an UTMA account?

a. NYSE stocks
b. Options
c. OTC securities on FRB's approved list
d. None of the above

82. All of the following are advantages to setting up a trust account, except:

a. More efficient transfer of property on death
b. Reduces probate fees and taxes
c. Avoids public disclosure of assets and transfers of property
d. Reduces estate taxes

83. Whose responsibility is it to maintain a "fair and orderly market"?

a. Commission house broker
b. Designated Market Maker
c. Two dollar broker
d. Supplemental liquidity provider

84. The "spread" is defined as:

a. The difference between the bid and the quote
b. The difference between the last sale and the current quote
c. The difference between the high and low for the day
d. The difference between the bid and the ask

85. All of the following are true of ECNs, or the Fourth Market, except:

a. Some ECNs will only accept certain types of orders
b. Participants in ECNs are called subscribers and must pay a fee to trade
c. ECN trading is limited to hours the markets are open
d. ECNs allow subscribers to trade anonymously

86. Which of the following is the least risky way to profit from a stock declining in price?

a. Selling the stock short
b. Selling call options on the stock
c. Buying put options on the stock
d. Putting on a Bear Put Spread

87. Which of the following is not a "disciplined" way to buy or sell a stock?

a. Market order
b. Stop Limit order
c. Sell Limit order
d. Sell Stop order

88. An investment manager boasts a track record of a 22% return over the last 18 months. What is the annualized return?

a. 1.22%
b. 14.2%
c. 14.6%
d. 16.4%

89. Investment managers with which of the following should be avoided?

a. Positive Alpha
b. High Sharpe ratio
c. Low Sharpe ratio
d. High Expected return

90. Which of the following investments would you rather keep in your portfolio?

a. A fund with a high time-weighted return
b. A fund with a high dollar-weighted return
c. A fund with negative inflation adjusted return
d. A fund with a low risk adjusted return

91. Which of the following is the regulation directly governing Investment Advisers?

a. Securities Exchange Act of 1934
b. Investment Advisers Act of 1940
c. Prudent Investor Statute
d. Fiduciary Investment Act

92. Which of the following individuals is eligible to register with the SEC as an Investment Adviser?

a. A newsletter writer who recommends stocks and gets paid by subscribers
b. A financial planner who creates financial plans and charges by the hour
c. An RIA with $70 million AUM
d. An internet investment adviser

93. An Investment Adviser must do all of the following after registration except:

a. Keep records of all receipts and disbursements
b. Keep records of all advertising
c. Keep records of all commentary on investment recommendations
d. Keep records of all personal transactions of Rep and Principals

41

94. Which of the following is not prohibited from registering as an Investment Adviser?

a. Adviser of a hedge fund with $125 million AUM
b. Author and publisher of a stock picking newsletter
c. A teacher who teaches finance and investing
d. An Investment Adviser Representative

95. The following are expected activities of an IAR, except:

a. Managing accounts
b. Acquire new clients
c. Answer phones and handle scheduling
d. Make investment recommendations

96. Which of the following is the best definition of an Investment Adviser Representative?

a. Someone who raises capital for a hedge fund from new clients
b. A portfolio manager for a private equity fund
c. A clerical worker for an Investment Adviser
d. Someone who provides investment advice at an RIA firm.

97. Investment Adviser Representatives typically have to pass which of the following tests:

a. Series 63
b. Series 65
c. Series 7
d. Series 9/10

98. Which of the following employees of an Investment Advisor would not need to be registered?

a. A supervisor who does not directly engage in any selling or advice-giving
b. A clerical assistant who only takes customer orders when the IAR is busy
c. Someone primarily engaged in fundraising for the IA, but does no advising
d. Assistant responsible for making appointments, filing, local marketing and advertising

99. The key differentiator to identify a broker-dealer from other financial businesses is:

a. Engaged in the giving of financial advice for a fee
b. Engaged in the custodying of assets for clients
c. Engaged in the business of effecting transactions in securities
d. Engaged in the business of financial advice for a commission

100. A person engaged in what transactions does not need to be registered as an agent of a broker-dealer?

a. Selling fixed annuities
b. Selling variable life insurance
c. Selling futures and options contracts
d. Selling brokered certificates of deposits

101. Which of the following is not a normal part of the registration application for a broker-dealer?

a. Applicant's financial condition and history
b. A recent photo and fingerprints
c. Qualifications and business history
d. Business type and place of business

102. Broker-dealer post registration requirements include all of the following except:

a. Minimum net capital requirements
b. Maintenance of all "books and records"
c. All renewal applications and fees
d. Client communications covered by "attorney-client privilege"

103. The key definition of an agent of a broker-dealer is:

a. Any person who represents an issuer in affecting purchases of securities
b. Any person who represents a BD to affect purchases or sales of securities
c. Any person representing an issuer to affect an exempt transaction
d. Any person who is a BD affecting a purchase or sale of securities

104. An agent who sells only which of the following does have to be registered with FINRA?

a. Term life insurance
b. Bank certificates of deposit
c. Exempt municipal securities
d. Selling any of the above requires FINRA registration

105. If an agent of a BD has no place of business in a state, but does have institutional investors in the state, he:

a. Must register with the state
b. Must register only with the state where he has a place of business
c. Is exempt from registering in that state
d. Must register with the state where he has a place of business and with the SEC

106. Who can discipline and penalize an agent of a BD for misconduct?

a. FINRA
b. The state where the agent is registered
c. The SEC
d. All of the above

107. All of the following are considered securities except:

a. Debenture
b. Warrants
c. Commodities contract
d. Variable life insurance policy

108. All of the following is required by the State for a securities registration except:

a. State filing fee
b. Other states where security will be offered
c. Amount of securities offered in state
d. Amount of securities offered in other states

109. Which is not an Exempt security under the Uniform Securities Act?

a. A community bank Certificate of Deposit
b. A Canadian mining company bond
c. A Florida municipal revenue bond
d. An Arizona public utility company bond

110. Which security is not federally covered, meaning the SEC has not decreed the securities need to be registered with the SEC?

a. A non-profit security
b. An NYSE listed company's bond
c. A NASDAQ listed company's preferred stock
d. Securities issued by a registered Investment Company

111. Powers of the Administrator under the Uniform Securities Act include, but are not limited to:

a. Issue subpoenas to obtain evidence
b. Investigate both in and outside the state
c. Issue rules and orders
d. All of the above

112. What will an Administrator usually do for the affected parties before issuing a suspension order?

a. Issue an order to revoke the license pending review
b. Issue subpoenas to obtain evidence
c. Present written findings of fact
d. Issue an immediate cease and desist order

113. Which is not a "punitive order" likely to be imposed by an Administrator for misbehavior?

a. Cease and desist order
b. Cancellation of license
c. Denial of license
d. Revocation of license

114. Among the criminal penalties and civil liabilities, which of the following is not a remedy available to the Administrator?

a. Four years in prison
b. $5,000 fine
c. Court costs and attorney's fees
d. Price paid for security

115. Which of the following is a proper communication to prospects?

a. Using the designation "Senior Citizen Certified Adviser"
b. Using someone else's research and stock recommendations as one's own
c. Using current clients' names and account performance as advertising
d. Using guaranteed products in advertising literature

116. People involved in which of the following activities may use the term "investment counsel"

    a. Selling mutual funds
    b. Managing money for clients on a fee only basis
    c. Reviewing and creating financial plans for clients
    d. All of the above

117. An Investment Adviser wanting to hire a solicitor to sell and solicit new clients, must abide by which authority?

    a. The SEC
    b. The state administrator
    c. FINRA
    d. None of the above

118. The single most important thing for an Investment Adviser to do when communicating with clients and prospects is:

    a. Be honest
    b. Disclose everything
    c. Keep records
    d. Remember their names

119. Which of the following forms of compensation are not allowable for a BD even if disclosed?

    a. 12-b 1 fees
    b. AUM based fees
    c. Commissions on transactions
    d. Soft dollar such as overhead and salaries

120. Which of the following may be compensated with "Incentive allocations" such as a hedge fund, where they receive a portion of capital gains from the portfolio?

    a. Agent of a broker dealer
    b. An Investment Advisor
    c. An Investment Advisor Representative
    d. None of the above

121. What would not be involved in a soft dollar arrangement?

    a. Computer software
    b. Investment research
    c. Office equipment discounts
    d. Stock bonuses based on growth of accounts

122. Where is the primary location of compensation disclosures?

    a. The adviser's form ADV
    b. The adviser's brochures
    c. The client account paperwork
    d. The conversation between IA and client

123. Which of the following is not a qualified custodian?

a. Bank
b. An Adviser's LLC
c. A Broker-dealer
d. Registered futures commission merchant

124. Giving discretion over an account to an Investment Adviser includes authority to do all but:

a. Withdraw distributions
b. Decide when to sell a position
c. Decide what stock to purchase
d. Invest in a stock owned by the Adviser

125. A good definition of suitability is:

a. What a prudent investor would do
b. Meticulous record keeping of client transactions and investments
c. Appropriate to a client's goals and risk tolerance
d. A low-risk, dividend-paying stock

126. A fiduciary is one who:

a. Invests someone else's money
b. Adheres always to the suitability standard
c. Takes on a legal responsibility to put other's interest first
d. Earns the trust of his clients

127. Which of the following is a serious issue in a commission account, but not in a fee account?

a. Selling away
b. Client loans
c. Insider trading
d. Excessive trading

128. An unsolicited transaction for a client can be problematic for an IA in what way?

a. Not suitable for certain clients
b. Could become excessive trading in a commission account
c. Investment doesn't meet the prudent investor standards
d. None of the above

129. Which of the following potential conflicts of interest is it okay for an Investment Advisor Representative to not disclose?

a. Family ownership of a recommended stock
b. Family works for company recommended as investment
c. Personal ownership of recommended stock
d. None of the above

130. Failure to disclose which potential conflicts of interest to an advisory client could be found to be fraud?

a. The possibility of gaining a corporate 401k plan of a recommended stock
b. Knowing that your broker dealer has a corporate investment banking relationship with a recommended company
c. Knowing that a company insider may be leaving the company
d. All of the above

Answers and Explanations

1. D: Cyclical stocks do well in an expansion phase, and value investors try and buy stocks out of favor at cheap valuations, therefore in the trough phase before an expansion.

2. B: The peak phase is where cyclical stocks are popular and richly valued. At that time defensive stocks are cheaper and should hold their value better through the contraction phase.

3. D: All of the above. All of these, and more, are the tools the Fed uses to "tighten" or "loosen" money in its attempts to reduce unemployment and fight inflation.

4. D: Balance of payments tracks a country's balance of trade as well as investments. The others are key ingredients that make up a country's balance of trade, whether positive or negative.

5. B: While all of these factors are influential, a country's balance of trade is most directly influential to the strength or weakness of a country's currency.

6. B: When the risk premium widens, it implies that investors are risk averse. Usually in response to concerns for economic growth. When this happens, safer bonds are purchased and yields on riskier bonds need to be higher to attract investors.

7. B: An SBA loan, and other loans, would be considered a long term liability, not a current liability.

8. A: Operating expenses are not considered in calculating gross margin, but are factored into the operating margin.

9. A: Stockholders' equity is equal to a company's assets minus its liabilities. Another name for this is net worth.

10. B: The P/E ratio is the quickest and easiest way to determine whether a given stock is cheap or expensive. This ratio is most helpful as a way to see changes over time and compared to history.

11. C: Changes in P/E ratios are constant, moving daily with the stock price. This is publicly available information and is not something the company has any control over.

12. D: A fund that consistently has positive Alpha is a winner. Usually this is best when risk is taken into account. You can get a higher overall return by taking more risk, but there may be no Alpha at all and that really hurts in a down market.

13. C: You would need to calculate the future value of that $100,000 at a rate of return available to you to determine whether it's better to receive the money now or later

14. B: The median is the number in the middle, not the average. Four kids are under 4' and four kids are over 4'.

15. C: The 3% return you could have had is the opportunity cost given up in favor of a potentially higher return. Opportunity cost being perceived very high is often what drags investors into the stock market at highs rather than lows.

16. D: Particularly with interest rates and yields so low today, fixed income investors have to worry about all of these risks.

17. C: While buying deep value stocks can be a good investing strategy, it does not necessarily help you avoid any non-systematic risks.

18. D: Purchasing power risk, or inflation risk, is one of the most overlooked and ignored by conservative investors. To balance this risk, they are often required to take on more risk of another kind.

19. A: Typically, EM equities are invested in simply for capital appreciation, not income. Income investors tend to prefer much less volatility than is normal in emerging markets.

20. C: Banker's acceptance is commonly used among buyers and sellers in different countries involving the purchase of widgets.

21. B: Repurchase agreements are primarily a private transaction, with no real secondary market. This illiquidity makes it very important to know your counterparty very well.

22. D: All things being equal, the tax free nature of municipal notes will result in a lower rate of interest, which after taxes are considered is likely to be competitive.

23. B: As the "safest" investment in the world, US bonds don't pay as much as any other type of bond, but this is offset by the superior safety and liquidity.

24. C: I bonds can only be redeemed by the US Government itself. They are non-negotiable, and are simply savings bonds, not securities.

25. A: A convertible bond that is trading exactly at the stock conversion price is said to be at parity.

26. B: When rates are falling, issuers have the opportunity to refinance their debt at lower rates, making it more likely they will call their older, higher rate debt.

27. C: Eurodollar bonds are denominated and pay in US dollars, thereby eliminating currency risk. This can be a great way to get exposure to overseas markets without worrying about the currencies.

28. C: The nominal yield, or coupon rate, does not change over the life of the security.

29. B: Fitch's, and S&P's, BBB rating is equivalent to Moody's Baa.

30. B: Simply divide the bond's price by the conversion ratio to get the stock's price. Arbitragers sometimes specialize in taking advantage of the discounts or premiums of convertibles compared to the related stock.

31. C: American Depository Receipts are the simplest way to invest in foreign stocks. These shares remove some of the worries of investing in countries with less rigorous regulations.

32. C: Common stocks are much more likely to have capital gains than preferreds. Preferred stock doesn't have voting rights.

33. C: The total return of capital appreciation plus dividends is 24.7%. $54.25 minus $45.50 is $8.75 of capital appreciation, plus dividends of $2.50 equals $11.25 of total return. $11.25 return on $45.50 is 24.7%.

34. C: A municipal bond paying 5% would double in approximately 14 years. 72 divided by 5 = 14.4.

35. A: REITs, or Real Estate Investment Trusts, are the best way for most people to invest in commercial real estate.

36. B: The Market Cap is simply the value of all of the outstanding shares. The market cap will grow as the share price grows, or vice versa.

37. C: Both the A/D ratio and moving averages are forms of technical analysis, not fundamental. P/E and P/S ratios are both valuation metrics used by fundamental investors.

38. A: Diversification is the overwhelming benefit of pooled investments to the individual investor. The expenses and performance may be good or bad, expensive or cheap. And ETFs are often not managed at all.

39. B: A Long/Short fund is a type of hedge fund, mutual funds are not allowed to go short, or "hedge" using other instruments.

40. D: Normally, an ETF will have far lower expenses as there is not a professional manager buying and selling stocks. Occasionally a UIT will have really low expenses, but that is the exception rather than the rule.

41. A: A shares are the cheapest over the long term, though they have the highest up front sales charge. R shares are only available in retirement plans, not for the individual.

42. B: Closed end mutual funds trade like a stock and for periods of time can trade significantly above or below their NAV. It can be interesting to observe closed end funds at the end of the year as there is often significant tax loss selling that can create large discounts.

43. C: While you may pay a 5.5% sales charge on a mutual fund investment, when dividends are reinvested in additional shares, they are bought at NAV.

44. C: In most ways they are the same, but futures contracts deal with commodities. They both provide a way to get exposure to an underlying investment with limited risk.

45. D: One of the primary differences between a mutual fund and a hedge fund is the ability to go short, or hedge. In a dangerous, down market, it's very likely the hedge fund will make money and preserve capital much better. As well, hedge funds may use "risky" and sophisticated options strategies as well as go very concentrated in a few positions.

46. A: Typically, investors will get exposure to more strategies and managers for greater diversification. While greater diversification usually means less overall risk, there is no guarantee of that. And typically, the fees will go up rather than go down.

47. B: Term life is the least expensive type of life insurance and is sometime called "pure" insurance. Others have additional features that bring additional costs.

48. D: A fixed annuity is most similar to a CD, and does not have the volatility of others.

49. C: The equity indexed annuities can make sense for someone who wants the security of a fixed return but needs the possibility of a higher return to keep pace with inflation over time.

50. D: One of the primary benefits of an annuity is that they can be used to provide an income for the remainder of your life, no matter how long you live.

51. A: The sole proprietorship is very simple and relatively inexpensive to set up and run. Certainly, there are other kinds of costs for this simplicity, such as unlimited liability.

52. C: A sole proprietor has unlimited liability. Limiting liability is a prime benefit of most other business structures.

53. D: An S corp is limited to 100 shareholders. This is often a key determinant in choosing to become and an S corp or a C corp.

54. D: The C corp has to pay taxes as an entity and shareholders have to pay income taxes as well, resulting in "double taxation"

55. B: With a low tax bracket and a long time horizon, muni bonds can be eliminated from this group.

56. B: While it can be helpful sometimes, it is not a necessary datapoint to have when developing a basic profile and objectives.

57. C: While matching for the risk tolerance, fixed annuities are not very liquid compared to the other options. Often, they are illiquid and may involve a penalty to get your money out before it matures.

58. C: All income minus all expenses leaves us with discretionary income. It is a good discipline to have some savings and investment a part of the non-discretionary income.

59. D: Modern portfolio theory is used to try and create a portfolio that resides on the efficient frontier, where the optimum balance of risk and return is obtained.

60. B: The random walk theory says that actively picking stocks is no better than randomly throwing darts at stocks, much like the efficient market hypothesis.

61. A: The CAPM uses the risk-free rate to calculate an expected return for a given security and a given risk.

62. C: Enhanced Indexing is a hybrid of a long-term strategic and a shorter term tactical allocation strategy.

63. B: The taxation of long-term capital gains is irrelevant to the decision to have an investment fund actively or passively managed. The cheaper fees on (passively managed) index funds, the belief in markets' efficiency (and thus the prices' perfect reflection of reality, without any mind needed to spot market inefficiencies), and the belief that managers cannot beat the market are all relevant to the active vs. passive decision.

64. A: Tactical asset allocation is more active, attempting to time the markets, or sectors, or asset classes

65. D: A value investor is most interested in buying companies trading at or below their intrinsic value, and selling them when they are trading above fair value. Benjamin Graham is one of the famous pioneers of the value investing style.

66. A: This is straightforward strategic asset allocation methodology in action

67. D: An investor who believes in the efficient market hypothesis doesn't believe that active strategies can beat the market, therefore they wouldn't invest in strategies that attempt to do that.

68. B: Regularly investing a certain amount into a fund or stock is dollar cost averaging, which allows more shares to be bought when the price is down and gradually build up a position over time.

69. C: Having too much of your portfolio in any one stock, sector, industry, asset class or even country is not the way to have a resilient and well diversified portfolio. Having a concentrated portfolio is another name for having concentrated risk.

70. D: For filers below the 25%, the tax rate on qualified dividends is ZERO! For 25% and above, they pay just 15%.

71. A: For individuals in the 15% tax bracket, the long term capital gains rate for 2013 is 0%.

72. A: When a company makes a profit, it pays corporate taxes. Then when it pays out some of those profits in the form of a dividend, the shareholder also has to pay tax on that money. This is double taxation of the same money.

73. D: To avoid a wash sale, you must wait 30 days before buying the same security. Otherwise the tax loss is nullified. Important to keep this in mind at the end of the year, so if you want to keep a position you can buy the stock in the company at least 32 days before the end of the year, assuming the last days are not on the weekend. You need to hold it for 30 days and then sell it still in the calendar year to register the loss.

74. B: A contribution to a traditional IRA is the only one that will give you a tax deduction. After-tax money goes into a Roth, and the 401s and 403s are pre-tax dollars that reduce your taxable income.

75. C: The Roth allows the investor to withdraw all money, both contributions and gains, tax free in retirement. There are also special provisions where you can withdraw before retirement age for a down payment on a first house, for example.

76. B: A defined benefit plan can work out well for older employees looking to make up time, whereas the others use time and compounding as key components. The earlier you start, the better your results will be with a 401k or IRA.

77. A: Unless of course the CEO is also on a committee or a trustee of the plan, he/she would not be a fiduciary.

78. A: In a Safe Harbor plan, you don't make recommendations, but simply provide an environment where participants are able to make good decisions for themselves. Having a good education program is important both to maintaining the Safe Harbor qualifications but also for the benefit of participants.

79. C: This could also be said as pretty much never, but the law allows for the possibility that in some unknown circumstances the clearly prudent thing would be to override the policy if it will clearly violate ERISA to NOT do it.

80. C: 529s are designed specifically for college costs. Coverdells are education savings accounts, but can be used for any age education.

81. D: UTMA/UGMA accounts cannot be set up on margin. They are fiduciary accounts, and margin increases risk.

82. B: Assets placed in a trust account completely eliminate probate fees on those assets, and there is no such thing as probate taxes.

83. B: The DMM has the responsibility of "making the market" and ensuring there is liquidity, especially during times of volatility. There has been much commentary around market volatility increasing as these jobs are given over to computers rather than humans.

84. D: The spread is the difference between the current bid and ask, and the DMM will stand ready to buy or sell at those prices.

85. C: Trading is allowed after hours as well. There are some distinct advantages for larger institutions, especially the ability to trade anonymously.

86. D: Selling a stock short has an "unlimited" risk. The stock can, at least in theory, go up forever and thereby there is no end to the risk. Buying straight puts is similar to putting on a bear put spread, with the difference being the sale of lower strike puts which simply reduces total cash outlay and therefore reducing potential loss.

87. A: A market order is an "instant gratification" order, not one that is planned, strategic, and "disciplined". More times than not, a market order is used by an amateur and rarely if ever by a professional.

88. B: The 18-month return is 14.2% annualized. This result is found by using the formula for annualized return: $(Return)^{1/years} - 1$. Insert 1.22 for the return and 1.5 for the years: $(1.22)^{1/1.5} - 1 = 14.2\%$.

89. C: The lower the Sharpe ratio, the worse the manager's performance on a risk-adjusted basis. In strong bull markets, many managers will try to add to their performance simply by taking on more "beta" or risk.

90. B: The high dollar weighted return is much more favorable than the other alternatives, as that involves the investor's actual return. It is similar to what can happen when investing in mutual funds at the end of a positive year. If you invest right before capital gain distributions you can end up paying taxes on gains in the fund that you didn't actually get, but you do get the tax burden. Obviously, this is not a concern in tax deferred accounts.

91. B: The fiduciary standards and references to prudent investors are contained within the Act of 1940. The prudent investor statutes are also referred to often in trust laws and ERISA laws.

92. D: An "Internet Investment Adviser" is eligible to register with the SEC. The others are not.

93. C: This is one of the very few things that IA's are not required to keep records of. Regulations are very serious and a bit onerous, so usually if it's asked whether an Investment Adviser needs to maintain records of something, the answer is yes.

94. A: Advisers to hedge funds are *exempt* from registering if they have less than $150 million in assets under management (AUM), but they are not *prohibited* from registering. Once they have over $100 million AUM, they may choose to register with the SEC, though it is not required.

95. C: These are not activities expected of an IAR, and don't require someone to be registered. Someone who primarily answers the phone, handles mail, and does not give advice or place stock orders doesn't need to be registered.

96. D: Most of the people who work in the advisory business at a registered IA business will be IARs.

97. B: The 65 is the normal exam for IARs with the other typical requirement being a combo of the 7 and the 66.

98. D: Anyone who directly supervises employees who engage in activities of an IAR must themselves be registered as IARs. Only the assistant who does not take orders would not need to be registered.

99. C: Broker-dealers are in the business of securities transactions. Often, they will custody assets, give advice, charge commissions and fees, but the core business is always transactions.

100. A: Fixed annuities are not securities and therefore someone only selling these is not required to be registered.

101. B: Considering a BD is usually only a "person" in the legal sense, there are no requirements for a photo or fingerprints. Fingerprints are required for every agent and principal involved, however.

102. D: This is a bit of a trick, as broker-dealers do not have communications covered by attorney-client privilege that can be withheld from the Administrator. Generally, BDs are required to retain everything imaginable to do with how they conduct business and it's ALL reviewable by the administrator in the interest of protecting investors.

103. B: The key is a person who is not a BD, who represents a BD or an issuer to effect purchases or sales of securities.

104. C: Even though the securities are exempt, the agent still has to be registered when offering and selling on behalf of the BD.

105. C: Given the information in this question, the only answer we can be sure of is that he/she is exempt from registration in that state.

106. D: Wrongdoing in the securities industry can bring the hammer down from multiple organizations. Although the media might paint it otherwise, the regulators are very serious and diligent and not very merciful when wrongdoing is uncovered.

107. C: Commodities and commodity futures contracts are not securities. They are regulated by the Commodities Futures Trading Commission.

108. D: They don't ask about the amounts offered in other states, simply the names of the states. This ensures they investigate and make sure there are not outstanding issues and actions taken by other states.

109. B: All Canadian government bonds are exempt, but not a Canadian company's bonds. Band deposit CDs, all muni bonds, and all securities of public utilities are exempt.

110. A: All non-profit securities are exempt from State registration, but they are not federally covered securities that must be registered with the SEC.

111. D: All of the above, plus several others. There are not many things an Administrator cannot due in pursuit of protection of the investors in its state, but it cannot issue judicial injunctions, sentence people to prison or impose criminal penalties, or make arrests!

112. C: The three things usually done are: give prior notice of the stop order, provide an opportunity for a hearing, and present findings of fact and conclusions of law.

113. B: A cancellation is a non-punitive action. This occurs when someone goes out of business, dies, is declared mentally incompetent, or simply can't be located.

114. A: Criminal penalties can be three years in prison, $5,000 fine, or both. Civil liabilities are in place to effectively make the investor whole.

115. D: The use of products with guarantees is fine as long as it's not misleading. Many annuity products with guarantees are popular and perfectly legal.

116. B: The use of this term is only allowable for people specifically rendering investment advisory services and or acting primarily as an investment adviser.

117. B: An Investment Adviser will either be registered with the SEC or the state administrator, but when it comes to a solicitor, the state administrator is the one that matters. Some states take the position that the solicitor must also be registered as an IAR, but it's not consistently that way.

118. B: Disclosure is something that cannot be overdone. When in doubt, disclose. Keeping records of conversations is always a good idea, especially of what and when you disclosed.

119. D: Soft-dollar compensation is usually okay for IAs if they disclose, however BDs are not allowed such things as office equipment, furniture, salaries, overhead, cell phones, and vacations.

120. D: IA's may generally be compensated on a percentage of assets over a period of time, and are thereby incentivized to grow the fee base, but they cannot share in capital gains made from investments.

121. D: Soft dollar arrangements are arrangements between asset managers and broker-dealers, where a good or service that the broker-dealer provides – e.g. computer software, investment research, or office equipment discounts – is compensated not with straight cash (a "hard dollar" arrangement) but with customer commissions. Hence the expenses for such goods or services are harder to trace and less perceptibly passed on to customers, leading some to question the practice.

122. A: The Form ADV needs to spell out all details of relevance, especially things that need clear disclosure such as how the adviser gets paid. Whether that is commission or fees or both, it needs to be accurately and clearly spelled out.

123. B: It is almost never a good idea to go with the Investment Adviser also having custody of client's assets. Many states have specifically outlawed this, and the others will probably do so in the future.

124. A: Discretion involves decisions over what to do with assets inside the account, and does not include taking money out of the account. Buying a stock already owned by the Adviser would be something that needs to be disclosed at minimum to the client, but having discretion makes such a thing perfectly legal.

125. C: Simply making sure the investment is appropriate for a client's stated goals and risk tolerance amply covers the suitability issue.

126. C: A fiduciary is legally bound to put client's interests before his own, as well as adhering to the Prudent Investor standards of conduct.

127. D: Excessive trading, or churning, is a problem in a commission account but not a fee-based account. The other things will cause you problems no matter the account!

128. D: Unsolicited transactions are usually more problematic for the client than the adviser, but the fact that it is unsolicited on the part of the adviser removes most of his liability.

129. D: As a fiduciary, not disclosing something that could make you—even unconsciously—give advice that is not disinterested could be considered as fraud!

130. D: Disclose ALL potential conflicts, both conscious and unconscious, to stay in the clear. As stated before, when in doubt disclose.

Thank You

We at Mometrix would like to extend our heartfelt thanks to you, our friend and patron, for allowing us to play a part in your journey. It is a privilege to serve people from all walks of life who are unified in their commitment to building the best future they can for themselves.

The preparation you devote to these important testing milestones may be the most valuable educational opportunity you have for making a real difference in your life. We encourage you to put your heart into it—that feeling of succeeding, overcoming, and yes, conquering will be well worth the hours you've invested.

We want to hear your story, your struggles and your successes, and if you see any opportunities for us to improve our materials so we can help others even more effectively in the future, please share that with us as well. **The team at Mometrix would be absolutely thrilled to hear from you!** So please, send us an email (support@mometrix.com) and let's stay in touch.

If you feel as though you need additional help, please check out the other resources we offer:

Study Guide: http://MometrixStudyGuides.com/Series65

Flashcards: http://MometrixFlashcards.com/Series65

Made in United States
Orlando, FL
08 January 2022

13174828R00037